Dear Crabby
You Asked, Maxine Answered

Copyright © 2005
Hallmark Licensing, Inc.

Published by Hallmark Books, a division of Hallmark Cards, Inc.,
Kansas City, MO 64141

Visit us on the Web at www.Hallmark.com.

Illustrations by John Wagner
Writing by Bill Gray and Dan Taylor
Editorial Director: Todd Hafer
Editorial Development: Jane-Elyse Pryor
Art Director: Mark Cordes
Designer: Walé Adeniran

Contributing writers: Nancy Cox, Amie Doyen, Scott Emmons, Steve King, Myra Zirkle

PowerPoint is a registered trademark of Microsoft Corporation
Jaws of Life is a registered trademark of Hale Products Inc.

BOK2057
PRINTED IN CHINA

Dear Crabby
You Asked, Maxine Answered

- Pets • Health & Fitness
- Fashion • Technology
- Romance • Aging

Illustrations by
JWagner

Written by
Bill Gray & Dan Taylor

GIFT BOOKS
from Hallmark

Introduction

People write me letters. They send e-mails. They fax. They may well text message, but since I have no idea what that is, I can't say. Which is funny, because I can say anything to anyone, mainly because I'm sure I'm as right as the rain that leaks on the screened-in porch.

Yeah, I'm kind of a Dr. I've-Had-My-Fill, and now I'm ready to slop some knowledge over on a deserving public.

You'll probably find a question or two here that have kept you awake nights. And even the questions that don't do to your brain what a burrito does to my...well, even the other questions will teach you something.

Yes, I think of myself as a teacher. "I'll teach you a thing or two!" is my message. I've forgotten more than most people have learned, and I'm happy to make up the rest.

If you've got questions, I've got answers. And if you don't have questions, I've still got answers. Stretch your arms out to reading distance and give this book a gander. It'll goose you toward being the best you that you can be.

Namely, a you that's more like me.

Maxine

Dear Maxine,

Technology's great, but sometimes I worry it's going too far. Should we fear artificial intelligence?

Overreacting to Robots in Boca Raton

Dear Maxine,

Can you explain the etiquette for using
a cell phone in a movie theater?

ON VIBRATE

Dear Maxine,
Do I need a phone that takes pictures?

Technophobic in Phoenix

Dear Tekkie,

Yes, you do!

You never know when someone will go 24/7 (which is putting a size 24 butt in size 7 bike shorts) and then bend over to pick up her purse dog! That's when the camera and the technology work together to do what our ancestors only dreamed of—namely, transmitting humiliation around the globe in seconds!

What a great time to be alive.

Dear Maxine,

Latte or Cappuccino?

Percolating in Peoria

Dear Perky,

That's a buddy cop movie, right? "Latte and Cappuccino—Caution: Justice Served Hot!"

I grind my own...teeth, that is, when I think about paying a jittery arm and leg for a cup of caffeine with a fancy-schmancy foreign name (not to mention a tip to a pierced and gloomy kid who can't wait to spend it on eyeliner). I've got coffee, I've got milk, and I'm steamed, so I can pour my own.

Dear Maxine,

My favorite band's reunion tour is coming to town, and it makes me wonder...when are we too old to rock and roll?

Groovy Granny in Galveston

Dear Rocky,

I say, rocking isn't just for chairs on porches! If you think you can still hear your favorite rock band, go out and see 'em as well.

Just don't think about the fake teeth, fake hair, and fake prerecorded vocals.

Take a little of the kids' inheritance money—okay, a lot of the kids' inheritance money—out of your 401, put on your 501s and a black T-shirt, and elbow your way to the front!

You might want to sell your car and get a beer and a hot dog as well. Or maybe sell your house and buy a souvenir T-shirt to wear to the next concert.

As long as these pickled relics want to jam, I think it's up to us to ice our knees and curl our arthritic fingers around our lighters and show our support. Or, if the mood hits you, lift that shirt and show them something substantially less supported. If that doesn't make 'em want to hang up the leather pants, I don't know what will.

Dear Maxine,
   It seems like you're always wearing those sunglasses.
   Is there anything you take your glasses off for?

Specs-tator

Dear Tator,
   Family reunions at the beach.
   Trust me, it ain't something
   you want to see clearly.

Dear Maxine,

Here's something that has me a little peeved. I put the newspapers out for recycling this morning, and they refused to take them because there was a magazine in the pile! I think that's unfair, don't you?

Trashy in Tallahassee

Dear Trashy,

Every day is trash day when you consider all the garbage you gotta deal with. And, unfortunately, one piece of that garbage is trash day.

Now I like to think of myself as a conscientious homeowner. I like to think of myself as a 19-year old swimsuit model, too, but only on the Internet.

But, yes, to answer your question, I think the trash company has too many nitpicky rules.

The console TV by the curb is "too heavy!" Take a chain saw to it, and suddenly it's "too splintery!"

The coffee grounds have to be in bags, rather than just setting the filters on the curb.

"That '56 Caddy won't fit in our truck."

"We don't take road kill."

"Technically, the bottle-blond, implanted floozy down the street with all the live-in 'nephews' doesn't qualify as 'trash.'"

Whine, whine, whine...

It's enough to make you want to go back to just tossin' the trash bags over the fence into the neighbor's yard.

Chomper Green
205 Recommend Avenue
Greenwich, CT 44530

Dear Maxine,
Seems everyone's into whitening
their teeth. Do you recommend
one system over another?

Grinning in Greenwich

Dear Chomper,
    Mine come out of the glass
lookin' pretty good. But when
    they need a touch-up, I've
got a little bottle of stuff
    near the typewriter
    that whites 'em out
        just fine.

Dear Maxine,
I'm thinking of redecorating with white carpet. Do I dare?

Floored in Florida

Dear Carp,

White carpet? Who are you, the Queen of England?
Get a dust-colored carpet. Or bring your dirty dog along and say, "Match this!"
Other color options are Mud, Sand, and Slush, depending on where you live.

Dear Maxine,
Do you use feng shui when you decorate?
"Feng" means wind, and "shui" means water. And after wind and water did a job on my roof, they're no longer welcome at my house.

Dear Maxine,

Recently I was at the grocers, picking up a few items on my way home from work.

I intended to use the "8 Items or Less" aisle to save time. When I reached the aisle, there was a woman in front of me who clearly had many more than eight items.

What should I have done? Contacted the manager? Addressed the woman directly? Ignored the situation?

TRAPPED IN EXPRESS

Dear Trapped,

Contact the manager? Are you kidding?! At most stores, that would be Binky. You can tell he's the manager because his "Hi! My Name is Binky!" tag has a lot more smiley faces stuck to it than the other junior high kids who work there. He got promoted to manager by being the only sucker who actually showed up for work on Labor Day weekend.

Here's a typical conversation with him:

"Can you tell me where to find canned tomatoes?"
    "Um...you mean the kind in cans?"
"Yeah. The canned ones in the cans."
    "Try fresh produce."

So, should you confront the woman directly? Unless you're the mayor of Wimpsburg, I'd say "Heck, yes!"

Remember your manners, and try to make a brief, yet concise comment expressing your displeasure.

Maybe one of these:

- "Pardon me, Miss Human Calculator, I can't help but notice you seem to be using a different system of counting than the rest of us here on Earth."
- "Yo, Roadblock, how'd you like me to make wine out of those grapes?"
- The sign doesn't say "8 Items or Whatever!"
- "You need to recount there, Einstein. Let me loan you a finger."

Finally, you ask if you should just ignore the situation. In my long and crabby life, I've found that whenever you ignore a jerkface who bugs you, it's like shaking a warm can of root beer one more time. When that honker blows, it's gonna be one fizzy volcano.

Crabby shopping!

Dear Maxine,

What do you think about flip-flops?

Open-Toed in Tonganoxie

Dear Maxine,
I'm thinking about playing the stock market. Any tips?

Bullish in Boston

Dear Maxine,

$40 million? $80 million? $125 million? How much is too much when it comes to athletes' salaries?

—Disillusioned Fan in Fargo

Dear Dizzy,

Before you pull a purse string, think about this. Let's say an athlete makes $10 million a year. Follow me...

Taxes take 50% or so, now we're down to $5 million. The agent takes 25% of the $10, leaving $2.5 million. Lawyers? Another 25% of the $10, leaving zero.

As you can see, you gotta feel sorry for the poor athlete who has to file for bankruptcy just to buy a single giant, gold necklace!

Dear Maxine,

I'm trying to find a good place to invest my savings, but I'm confused. Can you tell me the difference between compound and simple interest?

Invested Interest

Dear Maxine,

There's a lot of talk lately about executive salaries, and they do seem kind of high. What's a fair way to compensate corporate bigwigs?

Time clock Puncher in Petaluma

Dear Maxine,
　　Can you help me get along with a difficult co-worker?
Bugged in Buffalo

Dear Bugsy,
　　Follow my simple
three-step plan (and if
it makes you feel
better to put this into
a PowerPoint presentation,
then have at it).

Step One: Walk a mile in the other person's shoes.

Step Two: Make sure that mile includes
the boss's office, which you totally trash.

Step Three: Leave the shoes in the office as evidence.

Dear Indecent,
    Sure! I had a real thing for Sour Cream and Onion (regular, not wavy), then that cooled off, and I developed a passion for chocolate-covered pretzel twists, but they reminded me of doughnuts, so next thing you know, I came back to my first love, the greasy dozen.
    And it all happened at work. In fact, it's pretty much the only thing that has happened at work.

Dear Maxine,
   What can I do about a co-worker who keeps
   burning popcorn in the office kitchen?

Nose Holder in Nevada

Dear Maxine,

HOW DO YOU AVOID CONFLICT WITH LOVED ONES?

Easygoing in Erie

Dear Easy,

Simple—DON'T!

Why would anyone want to avoid conflict?

Let's take a minute to consider the word itself—"con," which in Spanish means "with," and "flict," which means "if you don't say what you mean, what you mean will be mean to you."

In other words, the people you choose to be with deserve to know what's annoying you. Particularly when it's their stupid, yappin' dog.

I'm shrinking, sure, but I don't shrink from conflict. Clearing the air is always a good thing. Especially if someone's been into the burritos con frijoles.

A Moment With Maxine

Where I come from, "fit" is something you throw and not something you try to be.

I've driven around the block enough times to know that sprinting around the block isn't my cup of carrot juice. And neither is carrot juice.

When I get out of bed at the crack of noon, the last thing on my mind is lacing up the ol' running shoes and pounding the bricks. I'm a lot more likely to slip into bunny slippers and pound a nonworking toaster.

Still, I have to admit that people seem to be endlessly fascinated with the latest health and exercise gimmick.

"How can we stay in shape, Maxine?" they write. Usually I recommend they take a long walk. Then I try not to point them towards the short pier.

Maxine

Dear Maxine,

Are you a jogger or a runner?

Marathon Manny

Dear Manny,
Definitely both!
If I'm not joggin' my memory,
I'm runnin' other people's lives.

.M.S Queen Mee
0 Health Nut Road
yramid, Ohio 74520

MAXINE
July 01
2004
LAND

Dear Maxine,

I recently read that they're thinking of making changes to the food pyramid. What next?! Every time I think I'm following a healthy diet, they go and change the rules!

What do you make of this pyramid debate?

Health Nut in Ohio

Dear Maxine,

What do you think of the all-protein diet?

Carnivorous in Calgary

Dear Carny,

Ever heard anybody say, "This party'll really rock when the vegetarians get here?" No. A diet that makes broccoli huggers cry is worth the trouble right there.

On the other hand, the right to bear doughnuts is one of our most prized freedoms. You couldn't get me separated from my dozen assorted with the Jaws of Life.

And if I try to eat a burrito without a shell, it might destroy the microwave.

Mark my words, carbs will come back, because diet fads are cyclical. Like doughnuts. Coincidence? I think not.

Dear Maxine,

Is yoga the answer?

Bent Out of Shape in Bentonville

Dear Benny,
Only if the question is
"How can I hurt
myself while wearing
silly pants and
no shoes?"

Dear Maxine,

What's the quickest way to lose five pounds?

Pound-Conscious in Portland

Dear Portly,

Throw away your diet books. Not only will you feel better, but you'll gain enough cabinet space for a deep fat fryer.

Dear Maxine,

I'm looking for an activity that provides both fun and exercise. Any suggestions?

Sporty in Spartanburg

Dear Sporty,

Well, let's look at some options.

Tennis? I figure if you're supposed to jump over the net when you win, you should also be able to throw your opponent over the net when you lose. Probably not.

Snow skiing? Nah...I'm already goin' downhill too fast.

Surfing? Hangin' ten reminds me that pretty much every thing I've got is hangin'.

I could go fishin', except I hate to hear people say, "Your bobbers are sinkin'."

Swimming is fun and good exercise. I'd do it, too, if it weren't for all the kids in the pool with guilty grins on their faces.

Treadmill? If I want to run all day without gettin' anyplace, I can just go to work.

Weight lifting? At my age, just haulin' my butt around qualifies.

I could try rock climbing...just me against nature. It's like drinking a large soda just before sitting through a movie. Plus, you get to moon everybody on the ground.

Actually, though, I'd rather ignore mountains just because they're there.

Camping? Pitching a tent makes me pitch a fit.

Hiking? If I want to feed the mosquitoes, I'll just give 'em a gift certificate to a blood bank.

All things considered, for fun and exercise, I'd recommend the Maxine two-step program.

Step One: Kick butts.

Step two: Take names.

Dear Maxine,
I want to live to be 125! Can you
give me any tips?

Hanging On in Ontario

Dear Hoo,

My answer is in the form of a question.

And the question is..."ARE YOU CRAZY?" 125 is too old. 125 is just showing off. That's 5 quarters of a century, and I don't know a lot about math, but I know that nothing should have 5 quarters.

I say, eat what you want, drink what you want, sleep when you want, and you'll end up doing something you enjoy. Isn't that better than spending your 125th year trying to find something good on TV? Believe me, there will not be a lot of programming for that demographic.

Living to be 125 years old is like sitting in a theater for an hour after the show is over. There's really nothing to see and nothing to do. Nothing but hang out with the other 125-year-olds, and all they want to do is complain about how their great-great-great-grandchildren don't call often enough.

Dear Maxine,
So, what's a typical Maxine day like, anyway?

A Fan

DEAR STALK...ER, I MEAN "FAN,"

   The alarm goes off at 6. Right after that, I go off on the alarm.

After eating a spoonful of instant coffee while waiting for my first pot to brew, I step outside to get the morning paper. Often the moon is still out. I gotta get better pajama elastic.

For breakfast I usually have poached eggs. Unless the farmer next door was lookin', and I couldn't poach 'em. I would have pancakes, but I hate to dirty a pan, so I just have cake instead.

Then I turn on my favorite morning aerobics program. After layin' on the couch makin' fun of those jiggling gee-haws for an hour, I'm ready to hit the street.

Some days I go to the mall and gripe at the sales clerks. Sometimes I go to the grocery store and gripe at the stock boys. Sometimes I'll visit a coffee shop and gripe at the prices.

Often my friends and I get together to talk about whichever friend didn't show up that day and to play a couple of hands of cards. Usually ca-nasty.

Sometimes in the evening I'll have a hot date. At least I assume he's sweatin' like that because he's hot. If I don't have a date, I might split a pizza with the girls. I like everything on mine...pepperoni, mushrooms, sausage, milk of magnesia.

Then I curl up on the couch with the dog and a good book. Right now I'm reading "50 Ways to Keep the Dog off the Couch." Unless, of course, the TV is functional. Then it's "Bye-bye, book!" After all, I have 300 channels, and somebody's always wrestling somewhere.

A Moment With Maxine

People want to know all
kinds of things about
Yours Grouchy.

I've got nothing to hide.

My life is an open book.
(This one, Sherlock,
this one right here.)

Just remember that
when you don't mind
your beeswax, you might
just get stung.

Maxine

Dear Maxine,
　　Which is your favorite bottled water?

H2O-in' in Omaha

Dear H2O,
　I like the kind with
　hops and barley
　in it that comes in
　the longneck
　bottle.

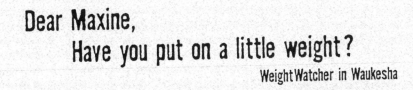

Dear Maxine,
        Have you put on a little weight?

WeightWatcher in Waukesha

Dear Pound Policeman,
    Have you lost
        the will to live?

Dear Maxine,

Are you a Democrat or a Republican?

Party Animal

Dear Animal,

I just vote for whoever makes sense. So I haven't voted since Thomas Dewey. Just joking. I think it's important to vote, even if you sometimes get disappointed. Like the time I thought "Hangin' Chad" was a candidate for judge. You know what they say..."If you don't vote, you can't complain." And how much fun would life be without complaining? Democrat or Republican? Actually, I'm more of a Crabertarian.

Dear Maxine,

Do you have a good treatment for the flu?

Rudy the Red-Nosed Sneezer

Dear Sneezer:

I remember the last time I had the flu. Boy was I crabby! Course, the two were unrelated. It snuck up on me like a neck breather in a popcorn line. I was at my desk at work, minding everybody else's business as usual, when I noticed a slight tickle in the back of my throat every time I tried to swallow my anger. I wrote it off as a lodged nacho chip.

Until I woke up in the middle of the night, honking like a Studebaker. Apparently the flu fairy had snuck into my room, filled my sinuses with oatmeal, welded my joints shut, and force-fed me a mini-volcano, which was rumbling ominously in my gut.

And, guess what? Every Dumb, Slick, and Scary had advice on a sure-fire cure for my flu.

"My grandfather drank a glass of garlic juice every morning! He lived to be 109 and never got the flu."

Yeah, well, with daily garlic-juice breath, I'm guessin' that's not all he never got.

"Vitamin C!"
"Grapefruit!"
"Feed the flu!"
"Starve the flu!"
"Moon the flu!" (My particular favorite.)

Nice try, folks, but everybody knows there's only one cure for the flu. Whining.

You will get over the flu in exact proportion to the amount of complaining you do about it. Heck, one of the reasons I drag myself to work when I'm sick is it's no fun to complain to the dog. I much prefer sitting slumped and grumpy in my office chair, bellowing like a wounded seal any time a co-worker comes within earshot.

Try it! Meanwhile, be sure to sneeze on everybody you don't like.

Unfortunately, the ship was less Baywatch, more Graywatch. Twelve hundred of us shuffled up the gangway and found our phone booths. Turned out those were the rooms. They call 'em cabins, but the inside of cabs are bigger.

You're not expected to spend much time in your cabin anyway, you're supposed to enjoy the amenities. "Amenities," if you don't know, is Latin for "pay extra." There are lots of places to drink, which might not be the smartest thing to do on a swaying vehicle.

And there are places to shop. The shopping is what they call "duty free," but they sure make it seem like it's your duty to do it. If you'd like to save up to 13% on a shell paperweight or a ship's logo tote bag that you'd never have bought at home, then the onboard boutiques are for you!

There are also lots of group activities. These can be avoided by hiding under a tarp in one of the not-enough-for-everybody lifeboats.

There's just nothing like living on a boat for 4 days to make the 361 on land seem great.

Dear Maxine,
Do you cook?

One Kitchen Babe

Hot Cross Buns

4 tablespoons sugar
1 teaspoon salt
3/4 " cinnamon.
Add 3 Tablespoons shortening
1 cup milk scalded and co
Blend in
1 egg well beaten
1 cake yeast dissolved in
lukewarm water.
1/2 cups raisins. - 4 or 4 1/4 cups

Hot Cross Buns
4 tablespoons sugar

heavy fry p.
both sides.
40-45 min.
more water if
Pour some c

white cookie
tter

salt

Dear Babe,

I believe the kitchen is the heart of the home. Or, in my case, the heartburn. It's there that I make all my favorite old family recipes: TV dinner, micro-wave popcorn, canned chili. For that special, personal touch, I'll occasionally even heat the chili, rather than just scooping it out of the can with nacho chips.

If you love your kitchen like I love mine, you're probably mentally picking out a drive-thru for dinner as you read this.

As for me, I'll just recall the hand-stitched words of the sampler that hung on my granny's wall: No matter what I serve my guests, it seems they're just a bunch of pests.

Dear Maxine,

Do you have a sleep aid that works?

Drowsy in Downer's Grove

A Moment With Maxine

When it comes to affairs of the heart, I usually just try to avoid EMTs, electric paddles, and the word "CLEAR!"

But some of you have questions about romance, dating, and relationships. I've got answers that may shock you.

Maxine

Dear Maxine,
A younger man is showing an interest in me!
What do you do when a young guy gives you the eye?

Flirting in Philly

Dear Philly Filly,
When a strong, attractive, young man looks at me, I know exactly what he wants. And so I tell him, "Put the bread on the top and carry the bags to my car. And don't hang around for a tip."

DEAR MAXINE,

What's with these old fogeys driving around in sports cars with women half their age?

Aged to Perfection

Dear Perfection,

Because men are lame. (By the way, Miss Perfection, you should write this answer down and save it. It works for a whole lot of questions.)

MAXINE TELEGRAM
KANSAS CITY,
MISSOURI 64108

Dear Maxine:

What's the secret to a long
and happy marriage?

Just Married in Maryland

Dear Naive Newlywed,

Long and happy? Sorry, dearie, you're gonna have to choose one or the other.

Just kiddin'. The real secret to a long and happy marriage is to accept each other just the way you are, assuming you've already changed everything about him.

Also, never go to bed angry. There's nothing worse than wasting a good temper tantrum by sleeping through it.

Finally, remember those three magic words every husband needs to hear just before he goes to sleep at night.

"In your dreams!"

Dear Maxine,
 I keep reading on T-shirts that Seniors are Sexy.
 Any tips for the mature dater?

Hot to Trot in Trenton

Dear Trotter,

   I believe the jury is still out on dating, but consider carbon. While it might not be 100% accurate, it should give you a ballpark figure. This is assuming that your birth certificate is a crumbly jumble of unreadable dust.

   I'm kidding, of course! Probably. But semi-seriously, Seniors who want to jump into the dating pool can avoid drowning in a sea of losers by following a few simple rules.

   1.) Never date anyone who lives nearby. If things don't work out and you keep running into your ex, it's awkward with a capital "awk."

   2.) Never date anyone who lives far away. Clearly, the problem here is that he or she is far away. The potential for the old "out of sight, out of mind" goes way up in your golden years.

   3.) Never date anyone who lives between nearby and far away. You don't want that kind of wishy-washy person in your life!

   By applying these simple rules, you'll find that you have lots of time to enjoy your friends, your family, and your exciting hobbies and volunteer work. Or...staring at TV and complaining about the government—the time-honored pursuits of the more mature among us.

Dear Maxine,
What's the secret to having a healthy sex life after middle age?

Still Frisky

Dear Frisk,
Learning to stand the sight of people your age naked.

Dear Maxine,
Do you think we need a man in our lives to feel complete?

Halfhearted in Hackensack

DEAR MAXINE,

My boyfriend wants me to get a boob job. What do you think?

To DD or Not to DD?

Dear DD,

I think your boyfriend IS a boob job. There's more to being a beautiful, mature woman than having a chest you can balance a TV tray on.

And if your boyfriend can't get that, he needs a nose job so he can wake up and smell the coffee! Or Double D latte, in his case.

Dolly Fhace-Surg
2000 Youthful Street
Hollyweird, TX 94620

Dear Maxine,
Should I consider plastic surgery
to achieve a youthful look?

Young at Heart, Old at Face

Dear Old Face,
Only if you want
to look like a
youthful astronaut
in a wind tunnel
experiment.

Dear Maxine,
   I try to eat at least one well–balanced meal a day, but it's hard.
   What tips do you have for healthy eating?

Whole Grain Granny in Cincinnati

Dear Grainy,
   Each day I try to enjoy something from each
of the four food groups: The bonbon group, the salty
snack group, the caffeine group, and the whatever-
the-thing-in-the-tinfoil-in-the-back-of-the-
fridge-is group.

A Moment With Maxine

I have one dog, one cat, and the nagging suspicion that I'm the victim of some animal kingdom prank. I feed them, I pay vet bills that could fund a small country, and I clean up hairballs and dog logs.

To return the favor, the dog drags me through the countryside with the leash while the cat is at home scratching Mount Rushmore into the arm of my couch.

When they look at me with those sad little eyes, I'll bet what they actually see is a big walking sucker.

So why do I keep them around? Simple.

Who else is gonna love you no matter how crabby you get?

Maxine

Dear Maxine,
    I'm in the market for a pet,
and I was wondering, since you have
both a cat and a dog, which would you
recommend?

                    Petless in Seattle

Dear Petless,

There are many questions you should ask yourself before getting any pet. For example, "AM I NUTS!? I can just barely live with myself! Why do I want a pet!?"

Trust me, some winter's night, when you're under your quilt and the dog is sleeping peacefully at your side, you'll know the answer to that question. Because that's when the cat will leap from the dresser and attach itself to your face like one of those sucky things from "Alien," waking up the dog, who will leave claw marks on your belly as he takes off across the room after the cat. At that moment, you'll know the answer to your question is "Yes, indeed, I am nuts."

But I digress. Often.

When trying to decide whether to get a cat or a dog, there's only one answer: Get both. Why drive yourself only half-crazy? Plus, that way they can keep each other occupied while you concentrate on the really big questions. Like whether to clean up the hairball first, or the dog log.

Dear Maxine:
How can I keep the cat
from shedding on the carpet?
Harry Rugs
Dear Harry,
Carpet the ceiling.
No, wait...that probably
wouldn't work either.

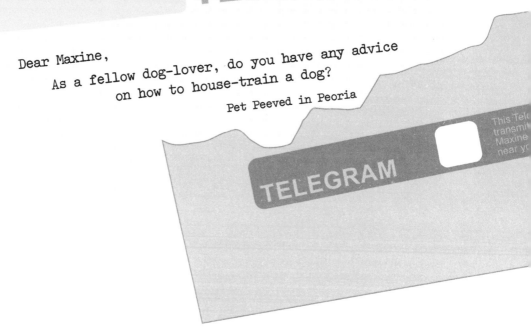

Dear Maxine,
As a fellow dog-lover, do you have any advice
on how to house-train a dog?

Pet Peeved in Peoria

TELEGRAM

This Tele
transmi
Maxine
near y

Dear Peeved,

First things first: You call me a "fellow dog lover." Wrong on both counts. I'm not a fellow, stray facial hairs notwithstanding. And I prefer to think of myself as more of a "dog tolerater."

Now, on to your question before I have to get up and let the dog out for the 100th time this hour. Dogs have to be trained to go outside to do their business, and I ain't talkin' a lemonade stand.

It's fairly simple to know when a dog has to go out-by the way it sniffs, whimpers, and barks once or twice.

When you spot these warning signs, you have plenty of time to get the dog picked up and head for the door before it dyes the front of your shirt a festive yellow.

Some dogs can be trained to go on the paper, which, believe me, works better if you're not reading the paper at the time.

One of the best ways to avoid accidents is to keep the dog from driving in the first place. Little joke there.

Actually, one of the best ways to avoid accidents is to take the dog for a walk every day.

The amount of time a dog must be walked will vary depending on how tired you are and how many degrees below zero it is. Apparently the little doggie-plumbing freezes up, since it takes a butt-numbing hour for the dog to find a place to go in the snow, while, if it's a nice night for a walk, it just goes on your front porch, then heads back inside.

As a final resort if none of this works, they make some lovely yellow carpeting.

Dear Maxine,

My doggie hates to take a bath. Do you have any tricks for getting your dog into the tub? *Dirty Dog Owner*

Dear Dirty,

You've hit upon one of the main differences between cats and dogs. Clearly, cats are better at self-cleaning than dogs. Heck, cats are better at self-cleaning than most people I ride the bus with.

Cats will spend many luxurious moments each day meticulously cleaning their fur. You will know this is true by two pieces of evidence: A cat that shines like the pants of a worn suit; and the big, sopping hairball that just soaked the bottom of your foot sock.

Dogs are notorious self-groomers, too, but only on one body part. This, of course, is the place-I-can't-write-about-in-a-family-book. Dogs have the cleanest place-I-can't-write-about-in-a-family-book in the entire animal kingdom. If you're looking for a whistle-clean place-I-can't-write-about-in-a-family-book, then a dog's your man.

But, back to your question regarding the best way to get the dog into the tub.

Have you tried filling the tub with meat?

With my dog, Floyd, I usually wait for a thunderstorm, then send him outside with a bar of soap tied around his neck.

Dear Maxine,

So many people have asked you so many questions. Isn't it time we got to the one, all-important, wrap-everything-up question that tops them all? What is the secret to life?

Searchin' in Secaucus

Dear Searchin',
I believe for every drop of rain that falls, a flower grows...and a foundation leaks and a ball game gets rained out and a car door rusts and...

But, semi-seriously, here are a few of the rules by which I've lived a long and crabby life:

- Try a little kindness. I try as little as possible.

- Follow your dream. Unless it's the one where you're at work in your underpants during a fire drill.

- Get along with people. It's easy if you have a positive attitude...and a black belt in karate. And if you can't get along with people, you can always tell those people to "get along" down the road.

- Remember, a kind word never hurt anybody. So, if you wanna hurt 'em, you'll have to try something else.

- And keep in mind that when all is said and done, most people still won't shut up.

So, to answer your question, "What is the secret to life?" let me just say...it's a SECRET, bonehead! What part of "secret" don't you understand?

Sheesh!

If you have enjoyed this book
or if you have a question for Maxine,
let us hear from you.

Please send comments and questions to:
Book Feedback,
2501 McGee, Mail Drop 250,
Kansas City, MO 64141–6580.

Or e–mail us at
booknotes@hallmark.com